DELUSION OF GRANDEUR

DELUSION OF GRANDEUR

A Poem for Voices
by Carol Hebald

Published by Turning Point
P.O. Box 541106
Cincinnati, OH 45254-1106

ISBN: 9781625491824

Poetry Editor: Kevin Walzer
Business Editor: Lori Jareo

Visit us on the web at www.turningpointbooks.com

Acknowledgments

Portions of *Delusion of Grandeur*, entitled The Fat Lady, appeared in play form in the August, 1989 issue of *Caprice* (Wichita, Kansas).

I am grateful to Dorothy Helly's Narrative Writing Group for their editorial suggestions on this manuscript.

My sincere thanks also to The MacDowell Colony where portions of this manuscript were revised.

I reserve special thanks to John Turner, whose technical support made this publication possible.

Table of Contents

To the memory of my mother

Canto One

Coney Island
on a Summer Sunday afternoon.
A slow Sun
is beginning to struggle
out of the clouds;
yesterday it rained.
The FAT LADY
sits in her Cage
like a clown,
the corners of her mouth
turned down.
Her hair is yellow straw;
she weighs four hundred
and eighty-four.
Fat flies buzzing around
settle on her cheeks.

In a neighboring Cage
a PANTHERESS
horses around in a dance
to the glee of a thin, gray-toned CHILD.
Each time PANTHERESS lifts her leg,
the CHILD lets out cries of joy
just like a little savage.
Beside her stands her daddy,
The IGNORANT/INNOCENT BYSTANDER
of thirty-three.
A strong growth of red, prickly hair
sprouts from his open shirt.
His plump wife plays with the penguins
down the lane.

In a Cage
on FAT LADY'S right
sits an ELEPHANT WITH TWO TRUNKS:
one tenor and one bass.

Diagonally opposite is an empty Bench.

An ORGANGRINDER and MONKEY pass by.
Ferries are tooting, and chimes have broken out.
A big beast of a pigeon
glistens as it struts in the Sun.

BYSTANDER'S CHILD

(To her father, regarding PANTHERESS):
Watch how fierce she is! She wants to play!

FAT LADY
(Absolutely furious with her competition, she
removes a mirrored compact from her pocket.)

I have a ten-foot pimple on my nose.

(She powders it, muttering):

I'll change that.

(Singing for her supper):

With a pimple on my conscience,
and a dimple on my cheek ...

(Calls out):

Step right up, folks!
I'll show you Energy,
heated by Emotion,
charged with the Will,
and directed by the Intellect.

(Disgusted by her failure, she turns to ELEPHANT on her Right.)

There must be easier ways of making a living than this.
I'd've become a hooker,
but I couldn't stand those goddamn stairs.

(Having overheard FAT LADY, BYSTANDER observes her
pocket her compact & growl for attention. As CHILD shrieks &
claps hands over PANTHERESS, FAT LADY steps Cage Center,
removes a slim dagger from her boot, lights the tip & tries to
swallow the flame, but it dies in mid-air. Finally aiming it at her

*heart, she catches BYSTANDER'S eye. He saunters over to her
Cage, & tosses her a peanut.)*

FAT LADY

Thanks.

(She eats it.)

Is that your wife over there
waddling after the penguins?

BYSTANDER

Yes.

FAT LADY

Well she has sick cats in her behind
and I hate her.

(BYSTANDER rewards her with another peanut.)

I not only hate her, I hate you.

BYSTANDER

(Poised to throw another):

Pardon? You hate whom?

FAT LADY

I not only hate whom,
I hate them.

*(She indicates spectators. Delighted by her
honesty, he is her captive audience now.)*

On top of which, Mister—

BYSTANDER

Call me Hermie, just plain Hermie.

(He hands her a brown paper bag.)

Here: you like pastrami? I just bought it—recently.
You'll eat later.

                              FAT LADY

Thanks, Hermie.

                              BYSTANDER

So what's the matter?

                              FAT LADY

I don't know from what to die.

               (She sighs, fanning away the flies.)

Yesterday I ordered my grave plot;
I figure I'm nice clientele.
Doesn't mean a thing anymore.
And the plot itself? Its location and size,
the quality of the worms,
to say nothing of the neighbors:
Highway robbery on sale.

                              BYSTANDER

I understand from what you say
that you're not enjoying yourself.

                              FAT LADY

Can you elaborate on that?

                              BYSTANDER

Who me?

                              FAT LADY

Excuse me;
I don't know who you are,
but you're terribly funny.

                              BYSTANDER

Kind of guy I am.
See, I understand you;
I hold a degree.

               (His CHILD wanders over to him.)

FAT LADY

I see;
allow me to introduce myself:
Miss Matzo, 1953.

BYSTANDER

Who?

CHILD
(Tugging at his pants):
Come on, Daddy.

BYSTANDER'S WIFE
(Calls):
Hermie, it's time to eat.

FAT LADY
(To CHILD):
How old are you?

CHILD

I'm seven.

FAT LADY

You married?

BYSTANDER

Take care!
*(CHILD pulls father off, as ELEPHANT hooks tenor
trunk over FAT LADY'S Cage, and pokes her with it.)*

FAT LADY
(To the dwindling CROWD):
I am the most provoking
still-life
you will ever have
the misfortune to meet.

(CROWD wanders off; she relaxes and sighs):
It's all right, I don't mind.
Rest is important, too.
And I like it here:
Everybody notices me.

      (She opens pastrami sandwich, gives half to
      ELEPHANT, who withdraws trunk and eats.)

A man comes here sometimes, nicer than Hermie.
He sits on that bench just watching me,
figuring me out quietly for a long time.
Then I catch his eye and we smile.
Later he gets up, excuses himself,
and goes away. And I just stay here all night long
and talk to the different people I've known.

      (She takes a bite of pastrami; turns to PANTHERESS):
You're not hungry, are you?

      (PANTHERESS nuzzles sleepily into her fur.)

Look at that!—Came out in one fur,
eats and sleeps in it
and she's happy.

      (PIGEON struts up to her Cage.)

You're cute too ...Yes you are!
Not like that scrawny kid with her daddy.
I was never scrawny, not me.
My daddy'd been dead a year
when I began asking strangers
on the street if they'd seen him.
Not everyone had time to listen.
They ran away from me
in the dead of winter, the cold.
Summertime was different;
strangers are nicer in the heat.
As a kid I loved the summer.
Those starry nights under the boardwalk
during the Second World War

when Pearl Harbor was the chick
the Japs attacked with their spears.
I used to kind of
roam around and wander up and smile:
"Lonesome, sailor?" I'd ask.
Some of them were.
So I offered to figure them out.
We'd stop under the boardwalk
and spend time, fool around;
it was nice. Some told sad stories.
One man bought me a jelly apple
"Just for listenin'."

> *(She bites into her pickle. GENTLEMAN/STRANGER enters*
> *in sunglasses and raincoat. He sits on the Bench, diagonally*
> *opposite her Cage.)*

He's come! He's come again
just to watch me.
If I could only break out of this Cage,
I'd sit down next to him.
But I wouldn't know what to say:
A my name is Alice?
My name isn't Alice!
I mean, where would I begin?

VOICE OF YENTA ANGEL
> *(From Above.)*

And he'd say *Nu?*

> *(NOOTSIE AND GOOTSIE ANGELS are lounging on a cloud):*

NOOTSIE ANGEL

What would you like to do?

GOOTSIE ANGEL

I don't know.

NOOTSIE ANGEL

Well, why don't we just
sit here and wonder?

GOOTSIE ANGEL

What would you like to wonder about?

NOOTSIE ANGEL

I wonder ...

GOOTSIE ANGEL

You're so lucky to have dimples.

NOOTSIE ANGEL

Lucky, you say?

GOOTSIE ANGEL

Yes; in fact,
I think they're beautiful.

YENTA ANGEL
(Dusting in GOOTSIE'S vicinity.)

Everything by her is beautiful.

FAT LADY
(Eager for company, she rises and addresses YENTA):

Excuse me; there's something on my mind:
it's really a problem I should discuss with YouKnowWho,
but He's sleeping now, so I thought I'd ask you.

YENTA ANGEL

Yes, what is it?

FAT LADY

Do you think my pimple will ever go away?

YENTA ANGEL

No.

*(FAT LADY returns to her seat and begins voraciously to eat
her pastrami sandwich, taking enormous bites and gulping
them down with diet soda. She stares straight ahead. Something
catches her eye.)*

FAT LADY

Ooolala! Ooooh—Look!
There goes my old boyfriend Lou
with his new shrew.
She's bald, he's sixty-two.
Watch them strut side-by-side
wagging their tails down the walk.
Elegant this afternoon
in radish-red on maroon,
Lou is discussing something *serious*
with her again, but as usual
Stephanie prefers not to listen.
Soon they'll wander home and wonder
what the sky will drop in the way of a drink
and then before their fuck
he'll tip her a wink just for luck,
her ardor old-shoeish as his ...

LADY FROM HUDATHOUGHTIT
(Passing her Cage.)

Well, I declare!

FAT LADY

What do you declare, dear?

LADY FROM HUDATHOUGHTIT
(To her husband):

What should I declare, dear?

(LADY and GENTLEMAN have conference.)

GENTLEMAN FROM HUDATHOUGHTIT

We declare

you should be soundly trounced.

> *(Announced with a twang.*
> *LADY and GENTLEMAN go off.)*

FAT LADY
> *(Finishes her sandwich, stands, and takes a deep breath.)*

OK—here we go:

> *(Pacing back and forth, she practices her singing exercises):*

NyamNyamNyamNyamNyamNyamNyamNyam
NyamNyamNyamNyamNyam.

> *(Growing vitalized, energized, she rocks from*
> *side-to-side, striding rhythmically across her Cage):*

NyamNyamNyamNyamNyamNyamNyamNyam
NyamNyamNyamNyamNyam ...

> *(Finished, she takes a swig of soda pop, and begins again to*
> *work):*

OK—Here we go:

> *(She starts a ragtime dance):*

A-toot, a-flute, a-bellow—What a dazzling m e l ody!

> *(GENTLEMAN/STRANGER rises from Bench and joins the*
> *gathering CROWD, the BYSTANDER'S CHILD on its Left. FAT*
> *LADY is really dancing now,—someone yells Whoopee! So*
> *carried away is she that she misses a step, trips, and lands on*
> *her buttocks: Jeers and applause from the CROWD.)*

FAT LADY

May I confess something?
I consider my grace
more a responsibility than a joy.

> *(Applause tapers off. FAT LADY stands up tall, and in full*
> *elegance takes a bow, as ELEPHANT emits a BLARE from*
> *his bass trunk. The disappointed CROWD wanders off.*
> *GENTLEMAN/STRANGER returns to Bench. BYSTANDER'S*
> *CHILD stays at FAT LADY'S Cage.)*

BYSTANDER'S CHILD

Don't feel bad;
you're not as fat as my Aunt Gussie.

FAT LADY

I'm devoted to you.

BYSTANDER'S CHILD
(Reconsiders):
Her thighs bulge more, but your busts are fatter.

FAT LADY
Why don't you join The Charming Child Contest around the bend?

BYSTANDER'S CHILD

I don't want to.

FAT LADY

Go, bubeleh, make a memory.

BYSTANDER'S CHILD

No.

(She sticks out her tongue and grimaces.)

FAT LADY
Are you just going to stand there making faces at me?

BYSTANDER'S CHILD

Yes.

FAT LADY

Why?

BYSTANDER'S CHILD

Just for spite.

*(FAT LADY'S attention is diverted by the STOUT, PIMPLY LADY,
who approaches her Cage carrying a used copy of Freud's
Interpretation of Dreams.)*

STOUT, PIMPLY LADY
Excuse me; I'm versed in you.

FAT LADY
Really?

STOUT, PIMPLY LADY
May I ask you a personal question?

FAT LADY
Would you?

STOUT, PIMPLY LADY
Of course.
    (She takes out pad and pen.)
What do you eat for breakfast?

FAT LADY
Pork and pork.

STOUT, PIMPLY LADY
Pork and pork?

FAT LADY
Two pieces of pork.

STOUT, PIMPLY LADY
That's all?
    (STOUT, PIMPLY LADY and CHILD fade from view.)

BYSTANDER
    (Sidling up to F.L.'s Cage):
How 'bout it?

FAT LADY
How 'bout what?

BYSTANDER

You know: *it*.

FAT LADY

It might
be a good idea
to give me
your left leg
as a pledge.

BYSTANDER

For what?

FAT LADY

For *it*.

BYSTANDER

What's *it*?

*(FAT LADY utters obscenity and starts laughing. The
BYSTANDER goes off in disgust.)*

FAT LADY

I cannot stop laughing—
sometimes I want to laugh
and sometimes I want to cry
but I don't know exactly why.
I'm not sure of what I'm doing,
I don't even know
why I am feeling. I don't know
why I'm supposed to feel at all
—I am entering into a symphony,
entering into a shrine.

*(Her voice trails off. MUSIC begins, swells;
GOD'S VOICE is heard as MUSIC fades.)*

VOICE OF GOD

I feel that You are hiding something from Me.

FAT LADY

Who's there? I can't see.

VOICE OF GOD

Tell Me your name.

FAT LADY

My name
is Never the Same.

VOICE OF GOD

Who are you?

FAT LADY

Nobody knows
so why should I care
why I am here
or why I am there?

CRACKS FROM THE GALLERY
(MALE VOICES as follows):

"Did *you* lay her?"
"Everybody did."
"How *was* she?"
"Absolutely marvelous."
"And so playful!"
"*Really?*"

FAT LADY
(Stepping Cage Center with a flourish):

Excuse me, gentlemen,
you're interrupting my train of thought.
I have healthy appetites:
Why you find it necessary
to remind me of that fact I don't know.
Why don't you just remember it?

(She stops, sits in dejection. BYSTANDER re-enters,
steps up to FAT LADY'S Cage, and removes wallet.)

BYSTANDER

How much?

(FAT LADY spits in his face; he wipes it off. Intending to leave,
he passes the Bench, and on impulse, crouches behind it. MUSIC:
A tune from a lone violin.)

VOICE OF GOD

Speak to me.

FAT LADY

Sometimes I feel
fire pure and simple,
an ecstasy from too much need ...

VOICE OF GOD

Why have you stopped?

FAT LADY

I can't begin.

VOICE OF GOD

Begin again. Begin.

(We hear the tapping of a baton.)

Speak in the Voice of My Blood,
sing to Me from the Sea.
I feel that you are hiding
something from Me.

FAT LADY

(Slowly at first):

In a ship on the sea
my lord with me,
my lord with me,
the sea was breathing

and my lord was dancing
severe, proud, clear as the skies ...
Still the music of those lips,
that radiant form.
The sea was breathing,
and my lord was dancing.
His eyes, mute birds,
beguiled me in song.
I saw in his cruelty
a tiny spark of mercy.

VOICE OF GOD

I see in your yearning
a tiny spark of hate.

FAT LADY

I am a large woman; praise me.

    (Pause.)

I was ashamed because I had hoped.
And Lucifer rose from the Waves
and beckoned me into the Deep.
And I danced through the waves
in a sea of dreams
and sang in the voice of my memory.

VOICE OF GOD

And the sun and the moon grew dark,
and the stars withdrew their shining.

FAT LADY

My senses curled to his dark body,
curled into his body
before he went away.
I've been broken by the Seas
in the depths of the Water.

VOICE OF GOD

Where is he now?

FAT LADY

(Points to Bench):

Over there. So dark, so tall ...

(LUCIFER, in sunglasses and raincoat, springs up from Bench, shields BYSTANDER from FAT LADY'S view. BYSTANDER aims pistol at her. MUSIC begins, swells, and recedes by the end of the following chanted interlude):

VOICE OF GOD

Life at its fullest
is merely a fragment;
the helpless flesh must fall.

FAT LADY

The birds among the leaves pure-calling,
leaf-stars whorling ...

VOICE OF GOD

His helpless flesh is falling.
As the body turns to ashes,
the Spirit mounts as a Flame.
Life at its fullest is merely a fragment ... (etc.)

(MUSIC OUT. The sun begins to set. LUCIFER sits hunched and shriveled on Bench.)

FAT LADY

I want: to die; I ought to die.
I am the Child of Satan.

VOICE OF GOD

You are a Child of Light.

(After a pause):

Little Child,
Why bother about the present?

You are the future,
and one must love only the future.

> *(CHRIST approaches her.)*

CHRIST

JoanMarie—

FAT LADY

Tell Him to go away.

VOICE OF GOD

He wants to speak.

> *(LUCIFER wipes his sunglasses, puts them on, squints, and jumps up.)*

LUCIFER

Why is it so bright here?
I hate the sunlight.

FAT LADY

Twice now He's invaded my sleep, thrown death into my eyes.

VOICE OF GOD

Who?

LUCIFER

> *(In extreme agitation.)*

I can't see! There's too much of a glare here!

> *(He sits; hides face from the light.)*

CHRIST

Father, make mercy in her.
Let her eat of My Bread
and drink of the Wine I have mingled,
and let her prepare her table before Me,
and anoint My Head with fresh oil.

LUCIFER

(Squirming around in his seat):

I want to insult the sunlight,
I want to *fight* with the sunlight.
It mocks me to misery—it glares, it glares.

> *(LUCIFER begins to box with the sunlight: it's a furious fight in the midst of which the sun blinds him, and he stumbles to his knees.)*

VOICE OF GOD

(To FAT LADY):

The Son beholds you sitting down
and rising up. You are His music.
Make Him songs among His jewels,
flee the fruit of lunacy.

FAT LADY

I cannot prove it wrong:
God speaks to me.

> *(CHRIST approaches her; she gasps, and hides at His feet.)*

CHRIST

Wounded in My shadow,
You must be born before you go.
Sister, take My Head a moment
to your breast...

VOICE OF GOD

(Echoes in the distance):

Make Him songs among His jewels ...

> *(BYSTANDER springs up from behind Bench, aims pistol, and crouches down. LUCIFER rises, and continues to box with the sunlight steadily, ray by ray, with such catlike precision he grows drunk on his own power):*

LUCIFER
I'll overwhelm the world with Pluto's blue fire!

VOICE OF YENTA ANGEL
(Heard from Above):
Oy vey! Do you smell smoke?

(ELEPHANT blares from his bass trunk;
CHRIST regards BYSTANDER briefly;
then, brushing past FAT LADY, disappears.)

FAT LADY
Hear my cry, oh Lord,
attend unto my plea.
If I must yet be stricken,
undertake for me.

LUCIFER
(Stalking her):
He won't;
in Him the Demon lies hidden.
And also in You;
And also in You.

FAT LADY
Fear and the Pit and the Snare are upon me!

LUCIFER
(Seducing her in a dance):
Not in hollow ease
will I be unremembered.
Sing, sweet harlot, sing!

FAT LADY
(Chants):
I hate the sunlight;
I want to insult the sunlight;

it mocks me to misery,
it glares—it glares—

>*(LUCIFER dances around her as she stands at the bars of her Cage shrieking cry, after cry, after cry. BYSTANDER fires shot from behind Bench; FAT LADY slumps forward and dies.*
>
>*ORGANGRINDER AND MONKEY cross in front of the FAT LADY'S cage; the MONKEY lies still; ORGANGRINDER stops, pokes him; the MONKEY is limp. ORGANGRINDER stuffs a piece of orange-rind into his mouth; then gently at first, then ever more fiercely, tries smacking him back to life.*

Canto Two

I

The Vestibule of Heaven. _Heaven itself is glimpsed through a
windowed wall. Although we never see it wholly, what we infer
is a perfect extension of reality in which hunger and desire exist
without pain. In the Tower of Babel, around which animals
graze, priests, rabbis, & scholars buzz with ideas; students lean
forward in rapt attention to poetry and music._

It is a slow time in the _Vestibule_; _one feels a certain tension in
the air._

_AT RISE: ST. JOAN is gossiping with the ARCHANGEL
MICHAEL, Here known as FOOTMAN FOOL, who stands in blue
livery at the Gate. Seated in the waiting area is the FAT LADY,
fussing in noticeable agitation with her ill-fitting, plumed hat.
She is the only newcomer in the_ _Vestibule_.

_YENTA ANGEL, the bookkeeper, sits at her desk, thumbing
through some notes. On her desk lie a ledger and a telephone:_

FAT LADY
(Rises and approaches her desk.)

Excuse me?

YENTA ANGEL

Yes, dear?

FAT LADY

I'd like to speak to the Chief.

YENTA ANGEL

I'm sorry; you'll have to wait.

FAT LADY
(Turns to find FOOTMAN FOOL in her seat):

How do you do?—Er—How are you?

(FOOTMAN FOOL glances about.)

Would you give a seat to a pregnant woman?

                              FOOTMAN FOOL
Certainly; where is she?

                                FAT LADY
Right here;—it's me.
I mean it's I.
          (Footman Fool rises quickly. FAT LADY sits.)

                              FOOTMAN FOOL
          (Confidentially):
Tell me: how long have you been pregnant?

                                FAT LADY
Fifteen minutes, but I'm simply exhausted.
               *(ST. JOAN tips him a wink to keep quiet.
               FAT LADY continues to fuss with her hat.)*

                              YENTA ANGEL
          (Finally taking pity on her):
If your hat doesn't fit your head,
we'll have it made smaller.

                                FAT LADY
Thank you.
          (Pause.)
Have what made smaller?

                              YENTA ANGEL
You know: *it.*

                                FAT LADY
It can't be taken in.

                              YENTA ANGEL
Sorry?

FAT LADY

I got it one-size-for-all
in Brooklyn.

YENTA ANGEL

I'm sorry?
What is your problem, dear?

FAT LADY

I think—I'm afraid I've been sent to the wrong place.

YENTA ANGEL

What did you say?

FAT LADY

I don't know. Please—
I don't know why I said that—please.

YENTA ANGEL

(Relenting.)
All right; come up.
> *(FAT LADY approaches desk; YENTA ANGEL opens her Ledger):*

Name?
> *(F.L. is silent. <u>Phone chimes once</u>.)*

Born?

FAT LADY

Yes, Ma'am.
> *(<u>Phone chimes twice</u>.)*

YENTA ANGEL

Sorry; I should have asked you ...
> *(<u>Phone chimes three times</u>.)*

Excuse me.
> *(She picks up):*

Yes? ...What? What was that?
A raid in the Tower of Babel?
Just a minute: Joan, come here.

ST. JOAN

What is it?

YENTA ANGEL
(With phone at her ear):

Some poets are storming the Tower of Babel.

ST. JOAN

With what?

YENTA ANGEL

With words.

ST. JOAN

I know! They began it early this morning.

YENTA ANGEL

Shhhah ...
(Listens ... reports):

They're challenging each other to
duels with words! They want a what? ...
A Universal Language to abolish whom?
Misunderstanding? Where? And, and—?

(TELEPHONE STATIC is heard.)

FAT LADY
(Freezes; chants in monotone):

I am she who is not,
daughter of the Father of Lies;
fire below, all fire within,
the Child of Satan,
my name is Sin.

(She gasps and hides her face. ST. JOAN watches her carefully as LADY STINGLEFINGER enters, exquisitely gowned, and jeweled.)

LADY STINGLEFINGER
(Elbowing her way past FOOTMAN FOOL.)
My son, who was an Elk,
has recently become a Muse.

FOOTMAN FOOL
You mean a Moose?

LADY STINGLEFINGER
Yes, I mean a Moose.

FOOTMAN FOOL
(Stepping into her path.)
Well, my Uncle is a Lion!

LADY STINGLEFINGER
Your monkey's Uncle?

FOOTMAN FOOL
Yes!

LADY STINGLEFINGER
And what does he eat?

FOOTMAN FOOL
He's especially fond of ...

(LADY STINGLEFINGER gossips animatedly with F.F. about food. Ignored, the FAT LADY cries quietly. ST. JOAN goes to her.)

ST. JOAN
What is it? What's the matter?
Are you really pregnant?

FAT LADY

I hope not. I don't know.
Help me!

ST. JOAN

What religion are you?

FAT LADY

None; but I'm born a Jew.

ST. JOAN

But your name isn't Sin!

FAT LADY

I don't know—I don't know—
Please! I feel so ashamed.
          (She runs away.)

ST. JOAN
          (After her.)
Who are you? What do you fear?

FAT LADY

I don't know.
I am not who I am.

ST. JOAN

What have you done?

FAT LADY

What crime?

ST. JOAN
          (Impatient.)
From where have you come?

FAT LADY

Brooklyn. Is it a mistake I'm here?

ST. JOAN

A mistake? Why?
How did you die?

FAT LADY

A shot rang out at midnight:
I knew I'd been hit.
I was working the Fat Lady shift
at Coney Island Zoo.
I must've died in my Cage. That's it.

    (Split-second pause.)

Please, may I see Him? When may I see Him?

ST. JOAN

I don't know that you will.

FAT LADY

I *must*.

    (JOAN checks her with a look.)

May I leave word for Him then—just in case?

ST. JOAN

What word?

FAT LADY

Send my desires as messengers
with a petition of our needs.
Tell Him this: my will
is a prisoner in His charge.
Only for love of Him
can the world be at liberty now.

ST. JOAN

Are you the child of Satan?

FAT LADY

I don't know—I think so.
But in me also is ...
Ask no more!

ST. JOAN
(To YENTA on telephone):

Her records, please.

YENTA ANGEL

What records? *I need a name.*

ST. JOAN

Who let her in?

YENTA ANGEL

Shhhh!
(Listens through PHONE STATIC):

What?—Chemical warfare where?
Where in the Middle East?
Speak more distinctly. I can't hear!

FAT LADY
(Again in a chant):

Help me to speak,
I can't listen and I can't speak ...

(She starts pacing through the Vestibule; *PHONE STATIC
increases.)*

YENTA ANGEL

I still can't—*What* is her problem, Joan?

(A BURST OF THUNDER. PHONE STATIC STOPS.)

Yes, I hear you now, I hear you:
Battles raging in Syria,
explosions of violence in Europe and the Middle East;
new terrors of anti-Semitism ...

FAT LADY
(Stretching out on the floor):

I think I have to give birth.

ST. JOAN

Does Our Father know about this?

YENTA ANGEL

His Majesty is taking a nap.

ST. JOAN

I'm waking Him up.

YENTA ANGEL

Oh, no you're not!

ST. JOAN

Oh yes I am!

YENTA ANGEL

Wait! Tell Him also ...

(Listens on phone, repeats):

About a crack plague
and a pandemic of child seduction in the Holy Catholic ...

(STATIC.)

BLACKOUT

II

GOD'S Chambers. GOD, asleep since the Holocaust, is dozing in
His Lounge Chair in a loose-fitting robe of blood-red silk. ST.
JOAN knocks softly, and enters:

ST. JOAN

My Lord?

GOD

     (Stirs awake):

Yes, Joan?

ST. JOAN

How was Your Majesty's nap?

GOD

I dreamed a memory
strange, troublesome, and long.
When I dozed off in '39,
the genius of evil was strong,
and I had just grown dim
knowing that grave massacre would come.
I stood upon My Mountain
immersed in Heaven past,
when a sorrowful, lonely old Jew
shouted from the distance below:
"How long will they oppress us,
and why should it be so?
Your cragged mountain lacks proportion!"
"You view it from below. Climb up," I called.
He took two paces, tripped a step,
and stumbling into prayer, cried out:
"Why have You forsaken us?
Where have You gone, my God?"
—I held a Sun on him.

Then drawing him at Noon
into the sublime and quiet regions of My Soul,
I wove him into the net of My music,
dazzled him in a dance of words ...

ST. JOAN
(Visibly impatient):

My Lord!
(After a respectful pause):

There's a lady in the Vestibule.
She's lying on the floor. She won't move; she can't.

GOD

Who is she?

ST. JOAN

She doesn't know.
I tried to question her,
but she ran from me and cried,
cried in such a way ... (*She can't explain.*)

GOD
(Pretends to nod off again):

Forgive Me.

ST. JOAN
(Groping for words.)

I think that no one has ever,
ever tried to help her stop.
(GOD fakes a snore. She shouts):

My King!

GOD

Sorry ... yes?
Tell Me her origin,
last place of abode;

nation and occupation,
the state of her faith:
Well? Begin.

ST. JOAN

She's an American, born a Jew,
last seen in Brooklyn
at the Coney Island Zoo.

GOD

How old is she?

ST. JOAN

In her middle years;
forty-four or so.

GOD

And what is her difficulty, Joan?

ST. JOAN

She finds it very hard to speak.
She fears—she thinks
she's been sent to the wrong place.
She claims—*(at God's audible yawn)*
Oh never mind. *(Airily)*: Probably
just another weeping widow, Father,
another stepchild of Your Majesty's,
convinced, no doubt, her misery
is greater than Your mercy,
and who has no thought
for the other things on Your Mind.

(GOD rebukes her with a sharp slap.)

Forgive me. You gave me courage
beyond that of most women;
I seem to make bad use of it Here
sometimes.

GOD

That wasn't always so, Joan.
Now what is the matter?

ST. JOAN

My dear Father,
You seem gracious at times
to some very peculiar people.

GOD

Joan, at times
I prefer you when you don't speak:
I understand you better.

ST. JOAN

A sweet reproof, my Lord.
I've only lately begun to study
and there's so much I don't understand,
so many questions I have
—though this is not the time.

(Again, GOD reclines.)

In fact, there's so little time.
Why, just yesterday in St. Teresa's class
we remembered how You preferred Us
to wrestle with You, like Jacob used to do,
to being surrounded by yes-persons
like a dictator.

GOD

Yes-persons?

ST. JOAN

I don't think You're really a dictator.

GOD

(Charmed, despite Himself, by her awkwardness.)

You don't?

ST. JOAN

Vengeful, and yet perfect, Father?
You don't really mean ...

GOD

There's more on Heaven and Earth
than is dreamt of in your—

ST. JOAN

Oh everyone knows that!
What *I* don't understand is why
the sins of the fathers are still
visited on the children,
when Auden himself says:
"Those to whom evil is done
Do evil in return."

GOD

A rather ambitious question, Joan,
when as you say, there's so little time.
Has Auden been quoting himself again?

ST. JOAN

No, Father; he read his poetry
after class this morning in the Tower.

GOD

Was Catherine[1] there?

ST. JOAN

Catherine left in the middle, Father, to pray:
She saw a lesser poet throw a stone at Auden.

GOD

Over what?

---

1   St. Catherine of Siena, His dearest daughter.

ST. JOAN

Over Auden's use of *evil* in the poem,
and then the Bishop threw a stone—
and a terrible ruckus began.
Catherine prayed at the entrance, Father.
She prayed for a very long time.

GOD

For what did she pray?

ST. JOAN

For the salvation of the Clergy,
and for the Holy Church.

> *(MESSENGER rushes in.)*

GOD

Yes, Gabriel?

MESSENGER

My Lord!—
There's a lady who came up
early this morning from Brooklyn
who had—*(Stops in embarrassment).*
She had ...well she was overcome
by a kind of nervous attack.

GOD

What kind of a nervous attack?

MESSENGER

A kind of intestinal attack.

GOD

> *(Losing patience.)*

What kind of an intestinal attack?

MESSENGER

A *gastro*intestinal attack it was.
—*Really*, Your Majesty,
my goodness—my!—
Right in the Vestibule.
It blew up a dreadful windstorm in Haiti,
and a blustering tornado in Kansas.
And then—then after her attack
she ran off to the Tower,
snuck in, and began throwing Matzo balls
around to all the Poets.

GOD

Where did she get them?

MESSENGER

No one knows.
She had two stuck in her hat!
But My Lord,
most awful of all:
She thinks her attack up Here
is causing the inflation below.
She holds herself responsible
for the energy crisis, the drought,
the shortage of fuel oil, and g-g-gas.

GOD

Who is this woman, Joan?

ST. JOAN

She doesn't know.
She fears she's the child of Satan.
She thinks—that she's pregnant...

GOD

By *Him*? Now she tells me!

ST. JOAN
(Confidently, now that she's winning):

She seeks You, Heavenly Father.
Her soul in utmost extremity of need
suffers a sharp martyrdom.
From the evil He did in her
We must labor with all Our Might
to bring forth good.
She is very much afraid.

GOD

Bring her to Me.

ST. JOAN

(Kneels):

Thank You, My Lord.

III

Early evening, the same. GOD is on His Throne; CHRIST at
His Right Hand. The FAT LADY, ushered in by MESSENGER,
trembles in terror at the door.

GOD

Child, what have they done to you?

FAT LADY

Is this happening? Is it true
or am I only imagining it?

GOD

You are imagining
what is true. Come here.

(He gestures with His Hand.
F.L. takes a slow step forward.)

Speak; don't be afraid. If I were not I,
your fear might be justified.
Who are you?—Speak.
Words distinct to Our Understanding
sculpt themselves in Our Memory.
Print them on Our Soul.
Do You love Us?

CHRIST

I fear she's too greatly moved.

GOD

Does the Devil's child intend herself so?
Speak. I urge you to begin.

(He motions CHRIST to help her.)

CHRIST

I hear a child's voice,
a child is trying to sing;
she wants to cry and she wants to sing.
I hear a split in the melody ...

FAT LADY

(Slowly at first):

When I was scarcely three,
"I am going to die,"
my father told me:
"Take me and put me
somewhere close to you."

(LIGHTS dim.)

I beside him long ago,
struck by the sunlight tipping the trees,
the darkness under the limbs,
took the vow of never-tell.
We spent his last year together.
I remember his great shout in the night:
"God, don't let me die."
Then, silence:
A candle in the window,
the morning sun shone red.
I wandered through his room,
his vacant room, and through
the different rooms,
I couldn't stop moving,
I couldn't stop searching
persistent at his door,
nursing memories at the window ...

CHRIST

When God, from the center of the sun,
spoke in a voice of thunder:

GOD

Little child, why bother about the present?
You are the future, and one must love
only the future.

    (Pause.)

Did you love Me?

FAT LADY

More than I could show—
how much more love I had—
I longed to live in a house on a hill
to be with You in a little room,
and never come nearer
the world than that.

GOD

Never nearer? Why?

FAT LADY

The authorities locked me up
as a ward of the state
because I grieved too much.

    (Recalls):

It was such a long way to Your Face.
I made up little songs,
I tried to pray.
Then someone began rocking me
in a very soft voice
and I began to swoon
but I needed also to scream.
I couldn't—do you understand?
I called; but no sound came out.
And I couldn't move until someone *did* hear
—do you understand?

MESSENGER

(Bursts in.)

My Lord, my God—
In Iran today the sun like a giant bullwhip
snapped shut the sky. The earth parted below—
and such grief as You alone have known ...
They cry in the Tower against you.

GOD

(Sharply.)

Tell them to prepare for the children.

(MESSENGER exits. To F.L.):

Go on.

(But she is shivering uncontrollably.)

CHRIST

(Strikes, steadies her.)

Say how you loved Us then, child.

FAT LADY

Loved You?
Consistent with Your mercy
was the mercy of the wind.
I struggled to reach You,
but You thrust me back.
I began secretly to hate You
because I couldn't understand You.

GOD

Had you loved Us then,
had you only tried—

FAT LADY

My God,
How often I cried to You,
Take me out of my body,

take me to the haven of light
—quick and sharp
as an eagle rising up—

GOD

You cried for your soul alone.

(Rest stop.)

FAT LADY

One day You revealed,
provided I always serve You,
the artist I'd become:
"An actress great and fine," You said,
"in the worthy theatre of Our love."
My heart was pierced by an Angel.
I vowed to embody
for all to comprehend
the minds and hearts of men,
the courage of ruthless women,
the lost cries of birds.
My soul upon my tongue
was drunk with love;
it uttered such heavenly folly
that Satan would suspend
my understanding from my prayers.
He said he had to punish me
and begged for my indulgence.
People thought me mad;
I felt myself so strange.
My soul tore in upon itself
with pain so great
no bodily torture could ever
take it away.

GOD

Had you no joy at all?

FAT LADY

Sometimes when You'd take me near You
for an instant, sometimes longer;
my body, stunned, lacked the strength to move.
My soul took it utterly away.

(Suddenly.)

Do I belong Here? Do I need a trial?
I could speak also at a trial.

GOD

You must come back again before
We let you know.

(F.L. starts to leave):

Tell Michael to find you
a rubber band for your hat.

FAT LADY

(Her hand on imaginary doorknob, she turns back in joy):

Tell who-oom?

GOD

The livery boy: Our Fool.

(Exit FAT LADY.)

CHRIST

She couldn't wish according to reason;
she learned to imagine from pain.

GOD

You knew?

CHRIST

I'd visit her sometimes too,
bestow on her the grace of ecstasy
only for the devil to intervene.
He woke foul dreams in her, he made her mad.

She'd dart from him in terror at night
like a fish snapping at its shadow.
After a time, she came
to an understanding with him.
He tormented her less.

GOD

Tell Me something of her understanding.

CHRIST

I let her see his misery in final clarity:
That cruelty, born of pain, tormented
by a longing for the Light. I urged her
to admit his presence within,
by her penance to appease his misery
and so absolve herself from sin.

GOD

What sin in her was gravest?
What deeds most cruel?

CHRIST

Sinning more in sentiment than deed—
Lord, let her tell the deeds!—
Most grievous and most grave
was her sin in being moved
by the sorrow of Satan.
Father, You loved him too.

GOD

Long before Your birth, I created him.
I yearned to see my Opposite
by virtue of Myself
still farther bring Me into Being.
Lucifer was born
and My Mind became a vast empire,
the Sea, His slave of longing.
I loved to watch Him brooding on the waves.

Dazzled by Our Glory, I Myself grew dim,
scarce discerned that Lucifer
had offended Me in sin;
seduced, in honor of His appetite,
My Virgin Queen of Angels.
I sent Them from My Sight
into the jaws of Hell.
I have no Child but You.

                                          CHRIST

Father, do You think,
this lady possibly could be
the very daughter of the Queen,
now by sorrow purified,
My Sister and My Bride?

                                          GOD

Your Mother's life in Hell
I ended with a birth—

              (MESSENGER runs in.)

I seem to recall the birth
of the girl child, JoanMarie ...
Yes, Gabriel?

                                      MESSENGER

              (Frightened.)

News, my Lord:
The poets were *stoning*
the Tower of Babel
when the clergy intervened.
And now—now they've begun
to bicker among themselves.
Who's right? Who's wrong?
Can no one up Here see
the other sides of questions?

GOD

What questions?

MESSENGER

How vengeance can be a savage form of justice
in Your name. Why the innocent are slaughtered
in Your name. The earth is going mad.
More men are threatening war.
False prophets everywhere abound.
And Lord, I fear to say it ...

GOD

Say it.

MESSENGER

Heaven Itself is on the brink of war.

CHRIST

Dear Father, call a truce!

GOD

I will.

　　　　(He exits swiftly.)

CHRIST

　　　　(Calling after Him):

Shall I come?

　　　　*(Hearing no answer, CHRIST turns to find that FAT LADY
　　　　has fled to the Up Right corner to pray. A silhouette of the
　　　　GENTLEMAN/STRANGER looms over her.*

Canto Three

I

GOD'S Chambers the following morning. CHRIST stands at the
window; ST. MARY enters, the FAT LADY trailing behind.

ST. MARY

Come in, Child. Sit down.

(She indicates a bench for FAT LADY to await her final
interview. GOD enters swiftly.)

CHRIST

What news, Father?

GOD

The truce began at sunrise.
My Saints pray at the Gate
while My earthly lords below
still fret their lives out,
now believing this, now believing that,
with new knowledge every day.
Some mean well
but seldom think well;
others think without feeling at all.
And of course the fault is Mine.
Here—even Here—
They call me a Malignant Deity.
Sweet Catherine told me so:
'Master of the Time Ceremony,'
I delight in baffling, in scattering human values.
Shall I dissolve the tie between Mankind and Me?
Their faith cannot invent me perfect—

CHRIST

My Lord—

GOD

—But like carping critics
sharp of eye, dull of vision,
Heaven is askew in them.
No wonder I sleep,
no wonder I grow dim.

    (He turns sharply to FAT LADY):
Well, my Lady? Speak. Why are you still?

FAT LADY

Of what should I speak?

GOD

Speak of the devil.

FAT LADY

I cannot, Lord, now.

GOD

Speak, then, of your sins.
List them one by one:
Begin.

FAT LADY

Guilty I *am* ...
First of the sin of gluttony,
and then, perhaps of lust.

GOD

Is that all?

FAT LADY

I think so; yes.

GOD

You were a voluptuary, My dear,
if you expected to rejoice Below,
and still to reign up Here.

FAT LADY

I didn't expect—
I didn't rejoice!

GOD

(To CHRIST):
Send her to Hell.

CHRIST

No, Father; may I ...?
(GOD signals approval for Him to continue. To F.L):
In what do you claim most proficiency?

FAT LADY

Most proficiency, Lord, in love.

CHRIST

Speak of that.

FAT LADY

How? My soul so often in distress
sometimes didn't know
if it was You or the devil guiding it.
I knew only
a pall of darkness
hid Your Light from me.
And then He sprang up everywhere,
endowing with divinity
men most steeped in sin.
I feared them to the bone,
dared deny no whim to them,
but made immediate delivery of me—
by all too quickly won.

GOD

By how many?

FAT LADY

Many, my Lord;
there's safety in numbers.

(Short pause.)

Suddenly, I grew ill.
My senses were sound:
with my ears I heard,
but didn't understand;
with my eyes I saw,
but couldn't perceive.
Suspended between Heaven and Earth,
neither to ascend nor rest,
I longed for final peace.
So hopeless it was
to try to control my mind.
I tried to die—not once, but many times.

(Rest stop.)

Locked in the asylum,
I was urged at first to speak;
I couldn't catch my thoughts.
They flew so quickly—birds in clouds—
I found only the air.

CHRIST

(Echoes):

Only the air.

FAT LADY

Soon I couldn't think at all.
The experts judged me lacking,
then asked me to respond.
I kept still. By their words,
no matter how cruel,
I vowed I would be healed.
Instead I grew much worse.
We tried to trust,

we prayed for faith,
we couldn't understand:
Is it so ridiculous to demand of a doctor,
to whom nothing should be alien,
that he be human too?

CHRIST

More ridiculous still to make of him a god
who gives audience only at fixed hours,
but seldom to the poor.

FAT LADY

Then I am guilty, too, of the sin of idolatry.

(GOD and CHRIST exchange glances.)

Discharged at thirty-three
on a windy morning in May,
in the garden I felt chilled.
A swallow skipped
from the limb of a tree
and flew over the high wall beyond.
And I heard my misery
in the crying of the wind.
My career abandoned,
finally I knew
the hopes that had fired it
were unattainable.
I took a job in the Zoo.
The rest you know.

CHRIST

Did you never think of Me?

FAT LADY

My understanding made no reflections;
it felt, could only feel.

CHRIST

Come, Child, come to my side.

(FAT LADY hesitates.)

Return, come.
The eye of your intellect
is sufficient to see,
your ears now to hear
the blessings of your King.

(FAT LADY advances; He kisses her brow.)

Daughter of the Father of Lies,
your vision darkened by infirm eyes
fix now on the light of Holy Faith.
Let the Blood I shed for you
deliver you now from Satan,
and by the wick that catches the Divine Flame
clothe you in the Light which scatters darkness.

(ST. MARY lights ceremonial candles):

FAT LADY

Tell me my name.

CHRIST

Conceived in Heaven,
born in Hell,
your name is JoanMarie—

(He sprinkles her with Baptismal Water.)

—My Sister and My Bride.

ST. MARY

And My Child, too.

(To CHRIST):

Your Sister's soul in flames
I quenched with my tears;
I gave her to drink.

(JOANMARIE kneels at Her feet. A commotion outside
is followed by MESSENGER'S swift entrance.)

GOD

Yes, Gabriel?

MESSENGER

Quickly, My Lord—come!
There's bedlam in the Tower again.

GOD

But I called a truce last night.

MESSENGER

They make a mockery of Your truce—
with what power I don't know.
My Lord, Come. Catherine, St. Catherine—

GOD

What of Catherine?

MESSENGER

She's wounded.

GOD

How? Where? My sweet Child—

MESSENGER

While praying in the Garden of Your Grace
an arrow sped into her entrails:
Who sent it no one knows.

GOD
(Glancing unconsciously at JOANMARIE):

What traitor here—?

CHRIST

Dear God, My Father, none!
But quickly stop the war.
I'll come.

GOD

You stay there. Come, Mary.
(They leave. CHRIST and JOANMARIE remain alone.)

CHRIST
(Peering beyond, then below.)

The mean high tide is rising,
the climeless moon is barking,
barking for another storm.

JOANMARIE

Is it my father who causes this?
Where is my father?
—In Heaven or Hell? Tell me.

CHRIST

In Heaven or in Hell
your father is too much with you.
Would you be merciful to him still?

JOANMARIE

No more; forgive me, no.
(Brief pause.)
Is he the devil?

CHRIST
(Smiles at the question.)

Who died when you were three?
No, that father is not the devil.
The devil isn't Jewish; he's multifarious.
And your father is not as important as Mine.
Yours was an instrument of evil

wrought from devil's agony,
and I am the Son of God.

JOANMARIE

And I am Your Sister
—and your bride.

CHRIST

Well then?
Where would you prefer to be,
Here or There?

JOANMARIE

I should be most blessed
in the lowest part of Heaven
for I have often been in Hell.
It's a great mercy of our Lord
to admit me at all.

CHRIST

Why?

JOANMARIE

My womb is still barren and full of thorns;
in the desert-places are wild beasts.

CHRIST

In the Temple of your soul is a Garden.
A Lamb is feeding in your Garden.
Did You know I loved You?
Have You ever known?

JOANMARIE

Yes, I knew.
Your humble sighs, purified by fire,
I thought sometimes my own.
I found on my hands and feet
Your very wounds.

(Pause; suddenly):
Will He send You again, my Lord,
to do mercy to the world?

> *(FLUTES, CHIMES, AND BELLS are heard from the Tower.)*

CHRIST
Why do you ask that, JoanMarie?

JOANMARIE
I feel afraid, as though suddenly a chill wind...
> *(She kneels at His feet.)*
Will you give me Your Child, my Lord?

CHRIST
> *(Steps back.)*
I?

JOANMARIE
Give me Your Child, my Lord!
Bind bones in me,
fasten my flesh.
Sweet Physician of my soul,
I don't want You to go.
> *(She kisses the hem of His robe.)*

CHRIST
But I've not been sent to go!

ST. JOAN
(Enters; makes her presence known):
Yenta has heard at the desk
and thought You'd like to know:
His Majesty has ended the war.

CHRIST
When?

ST. JOAN

Only a moment ago.
He'll stay a while with Catherine
till she's healed.

>*(JOANMARIE rises.)*

YENTA ANGEL
>*(Peers in; to ST. JOAN):*

It's time to lower the flame on the soup.

CHRIST

What soup?

YENTA ANGEL

My matzo ball soup.

ST. JOAN

Try it, You'll like it!

CHRIST

When—now?

ST. JOAN

Not so soon.
At the wedding upstairs
tomorrow at Noon.

CHRIST

For whom?

>*(ST. JOAN and JOANMARIE exchange smiles.)*

This is so—so—

YENTA ANGEL

Nu?

II

An *Indoor* and *Outdoor* wedding masquerade.

Outdoors: A mock Garden of Eden. Currents of leaves in filtered light shade a sculpture of Adam and Eve by the fountain. Center is the *Huppah*, a wedding canopy garlanded with roses, tulips, and carnations, around which CHRIST paces nervously up and down, as if waiting for a race to begin.

The GUESTS mill about: a mass of yarmulkes, top hats, and tulle. Several buzz around a large *Center Table* upon which rest dishes of shrimp fat as cherubs, gefilte fish, chicken soup with kreplach, a roast duckling; a tsimes, and little fluted balls of butter atop the strudel.

Indoors: *Center* is The Holy Throne. On Its Base are bas-reliefs of BIRDS, FROGS, & PENGUINS.

JOANMARIE, on the arm of GOD, approaches the *Huppah*, her face lit up with pride, apprehension, and joy. YENTA ANGEL scampers behind to pick up her train and twice trips over it, when suddenly a PENGUIN leaps out from the Base of GOD'S Throne and waddles toward JOANMARIE.

YENTA ANGEL
Where did *that* come from?

ST. MICHAEL
I saw it leap out from His Majesty's Throne!

YENTA ANGEL
Quick: Take it to the Zoo.

(As the GUESTS gather for the Outdoor Ceremony, ST. MICHAEL catches hold of PENGUIN, and turns it upside down to ascertain its sex; DAME PENGUIN screams and runs away. Her bill is black, and bright as jet; a red sash runs round her flippers and white chest; she, with the loveliest dyes upon her throat, resembles the gracious Lady Pertelote. Shyly she preens

*her feathers, glimpses her persecutor, then preens herself
some more. She sneaks a peek at the adoring Congregation. So
overcome is she by their admiration, that the feathers round
her throat puff out; she lowers her head demurely into them,
sits still, then gazes up at ST. MICHAEL. Catching a look of
tenderness in his eyes, she waddles towards him. He lowers
himself deftly to the ground, the better to catch hold of her. Then:
high up on her toes, her slender neck outstretched, eyes closed,
she clasps her beak upon his nose, and pulls and pulls and
pulls.—A sudden intake of breath causes her release. She topples
over on her back. He catches her, and sneaking her a sliver of
gefilte fish, rushes her off to the zoo.)*

GOD
(Under the Huppah with Bride & Groom.)
Speak of your love, JoanMarie.

JOANMARIE
I am unworthy, my Lord.

GOD
Speak again.

JOANMARIE
His glance before me,
His words in my ears,
He makes me see
how much of what I saw
I never saw at all.

*(She stops, distracted by the entrance of the GENTLEMAN/
STRANGER, disguised as a wolf in mouton lamb. GOD gestures
CHRIST to speak.)*

CHRIST
The eye of our intellect
ravished by fire

in striking purity burns
now with a brilliance infused.

  (Stops; He, too, sees the GENTLEMAN/STRANGER.)

JOANMARIE

  (Kneels; kisses CHRIST'S hem.)

I am in sweet bondage to my Lord.

GOD

  (Hands her a glass of wine):

From the well of His wisdom,
drink deep refreshment, Child.

  (She drinks, passes the glass to CHRIST, Who shatters it
  with His heel to loud cries of Mazel Tov. The GENTLEMAN/
  STRANGER hops to the <u>Huppah</u> to kiss the bride. JOANMARIE,
  startled, jumps away.)

STRANGER

  (At her heels.)

Do you know who I am?

JOANMARIE

  (Tries in vain to remember):

No; but if you check at the front desk,
I'm sure they'll be able to tell you.

  (GOD returns to His Throne. CHRIST and JOANMARIE wander
  off alone. The GENTLEMAN/STRANGER approaches the
  Throne; kneeling at its Base, he catches GOD'S eye, then turns
  sharply away.

  <u>Outside </u>in the garden a lone cherub sings: "A fig for doubts and
  fears. Hey, ding-a-ling." At <u>Center Table </u>a RABBI and a PRIEST
  grab for the same succulent slice of gefilte fish. The PRIEST wins
  it.)

RABBI

(Pleasantly.)

The visionary fish
I cannot dine on
I call unreal.

PRIEST

Were it truly unreal,
you would not.

    (He eats with relish. The following guests, with illuminated
    <u>name tags</u>, *join the clergy at Table.)*

THEODORE ROETHKE
(Forking a slice of fish, he addresses T. S. ELIOT):

These heavenly fish exist
so they may swim fictitious,
but fictitious fish can't swim
in leaky definitions
wrought by lexicographers,
inglorious and grim.

ELIOT

Don't be naughty, Teddy;
without them, where would the language be?

    (EMILY DICKINSON strolls by on KAFKA'S arm.)

DICKINSON

Which language do you mean? What say you, gossips?

    (KAFKA samples the soup.)

ROETHKE

Whichever one should be.

KAFKA

(Mutters.)

Too much salt, too much salt.

DICKINSON

And which one is that?

SHAKESPEARE

A language of feeling, a language of silence.

EINSTEIN

And one of science, too.

MARTIN LUTHER KING

Yet still of prayer.

BACH

A language of music.

BEETHOVEN

A language of passion.

WALLACE STEVENS
(Doffing his plumed hat):

Erudite and debonair.

ST. CATHERINE
(Softly.)

But mustn't it also be true?

STEVENS

True to what, yet true to whom?

ST. CATHERINE

True to His very Word.

STEVENS

I ain't a Saint, I'm just a Seer.

SHAKESPEARE

But what of the words we hear?

ST. CATHERINE

Need we have words at all?

DANTE

How otherwise can it be?

SOCRATES

Yes, how can it otherwise be,
if in the beginning was the Word?

ST. TERESA

But what must the words evoke?
Yes, what must they first evoke?

> *(The heated discussion culminates in a dance choreographed
> as a peripatetic argument, in which each luminary makes
> his/her point within the circle. The argument fades into
> silence.*
>
> Indoors: *The GENTLEMAN/STRANGER, still kneeling
> at Holy Throne, rises and stands before GOD,
> Whose Eyes are on him):*

GOD

Well?

G/STRANGER

(Bursts out):

What are You doing, my God Almighty?
Will You give blessing to my child
Through the seed of Your son?

GOD

Who are you?

G/STRANGER

You know who I am.
Father of the bride,
I dwelled with her Below.

GOD

Is it you, Lucifer?
Is it really ...?

G/STRANGER

Your Lordship, I.

GOD

When did you get Here? *How?*

G/STRANGER

(Bows profoundly.)
Master, I followed My heart.

GOD

You humble yourself in great pride.

G/STRANGER

(Rising slowly.)
Not without reason.
Long ago when I
took Mary from the Angels
into the bowels of hell
a daughter was born to Us
to atone by forever dying:
For Our sin her waking death.
Lord, what penance You exact.
When You brought Mary back
as Mother to Your Son,
My child remained in Hell
—and suffered at Our hands,
she suffered so ...

(He winces at the memory.)

GOD

Stay!—Speak more.
That child now is Here.
Why are You?

G/STRANGER

Kill Me; do mercy to the world
or send Your Son again.

GOD

My Son, Your child's Bridegroom
send from Us again?
Why now?

G/STRANGER

In death, free will is bound.
Kill Me; I cannot help torment.
The earth is full of war,
famine and disease.
Kill Me: I'm sick of Hell.

GOD

Hell has no power Here.
What is Your complaint?

G/STRANGER

I loved My child so
but found no way to hold her;
when I kept her in confusion,
she'd rise to Heaven on wings of mercy;
when You lifted her on High,
she'd humble herself down to Hell
and when I followed her There
she'd persecute Me so,
so lacerate My soul—

GOD

You're free of her now.

G/STRANGER

(Wistfully.)

She's over there ...I'm her father.

GOD

And I her Father-in-Law.

G/STRANGER

But Me she called her father from first birth,
and took such bliss with Me on Earth
that lent Us secret Heaven.

GOD

And kept her down in hell.

(Brief pause.)

G/STRANGER

Your Grace,
nothing is improper these days;
but—yet—

GOD

Well?

G/STRANGER

Your Son has married His Sister;
such marriages offend the Church.

GOD

Heaven is higher than the Church.
Here all things are possible,
all things exist.

G/STRANGER

(Sadly.)

All save I.
You brought Me into being;
once You loved Me too.

Love Me once again—or set Me free.
I'd tread the outskirts Here,
No more an enemy,—
a distant cousin to the spheres.
Only give Me a place to be!
I had one once at Your left hand
before You sent Me down.
I never could forget
the way You'd joust with Me:
Put questions on the cross of thought
to pluck a thought apart,
equal Yours to Mine...

      (Moved, GOD looks off into the Garden at the Sculptures of
      Adam and Eve. GENTLEMAN/STRANGER follows His gaze.)

GOD

(Quietly.)
I cannot; not again.

G/STRANGER

Look: Your first-born pray by the Fountain,
Once rebels just like Me,
gemmed in the Garden of Your Grace;
statues now, mere effigies.

GOD

Do you care for them still? Don't lie.

G/STRANGER

I care better for my child.

GOD

Damn You! She's My child now:
Let her be.
Would you drive her mad again from agony?
No angel, only a brute beast—

G/STRANGER

Stop! My Lord, I must confess
had You better understood Me,
I'd have tormented less.
Chain Me to that Fountain;
forbid Me to sin again,
forbid Me once again.
We are almost at war, My Lord,
yet We're longing to embrace.
Hold Me in bondage, keep Me.
I cannot help torment.

GOD

Then go!—I urge You to grieve
chained to the shadows of Adam and Eve;
soothe their disordered senses, cleanse them.
But You, from parching thirst,
will begin a quiet dying,
never to be renewed:
Your hand will reach for water,
return to Your lips,
and suddenly lock in air.
A shower will fall on You
from which You may drink a drop or two.
Twelve drops will sink You
into a soundless sleep
for the restoration of your soul.

G/STRANGER

For how long, My Lord?

GOD

For a thousand years, My Angel.

G/STRANGER

And will You always watch Me?

GOD

You'll not be gone from My sight.

G/STRANGER

And those sudden furies
wrung from Me by mere disharmony
no more will cause the Earth to quake,
volcanoes to erupt?
Will she see Me, Lord, before I sleep?

GOD

She'll never see you again.

G/STRANGER

Yet when she passes Me?

GOD

Invisible, You may see.
Go, now.

> *(G/STRANGER exits to Garden. At GOD'S bidding, GABRIEL
> chains Him to the Statues. CHRIST and JOANMARIE, seeing
> GOD in deep sorrow, go to Him.)*

CHRIST

Father, why do You weep?

GOD

Again You must go.
Again ...You must.

CHRIST

She feared it. JoanMarie!—

JOANMARIE

Give Me Your Child, My Lord.

> *(She catches the hem of His gown.)*

CHRIST

(To GOD):

Why now must I go?
Why more must she grieve?

JOANMARIE

Life was greater than death,
hope than despair,
when Sarah, across the centuries,
conceived.

CHRIST

I can give you no child, JoanMarie.
Exceeding sex means surpassing it,
having progeny by the spirit.

JOANMARIE

I'm not yet ready for that.

CHRIST

Dear Sister, you are.
I am the Immaculate Conception;
by yours Our Mother was stained.
Between your conception and Mine,
She suffered a rebirth Below
very like yours Here.
Go to Her, now.

JOANMARIE
(Moves toward ST. MARY; then turns to GOD):

When must He leave?

GOD

Tomorrow at Noon.

*(JOANMARIE, overcome, embraces the feet of the VIRGIN;
CHRIST'S gaze is on them. He glances back; GOD motions*

Him to let them weep. FATHER & SON look into the Garden
at the statues of Adam & Eve.)

CHRIST

Forested in memory
they are together.
They obey Your silence...

(He sees the STRANGER.)

Father, there's a gentleman
chained in the shadows
I saw Here earlier today.

GOD

It's her first Father, Son.
She doesn't know he's there.

CHRIST

I know now why I must go.

(He crosses back to JOANMARIE):

Virtue, the Nurse to feed you,
has blood in Her breast, has milk.
In the shadows and between them,
think only of Me.
Accept this token of mourning love.

(He offers her <u>Rosary Beads</u>.)

JOANMARIE

(Takes them; rises):

My Lord, My God,
may I go with Him to Earth?

GOD

Not yet, JoanMarie.
He'll send for you one day.
Perhaps He will send.

(JOANMARIE kneels at the Left Hand of GOD and counts <u>Beads</u>; CHRIST prays at GOD'S Right. The VIRGIN looks into the Garden.

LIGHTS FLOOD TO SUNSET. FOOTMAN FOOL re-enters with the PENGUIN as the band plays: "When the Saints Come Marching In."

YENTA ANGEL
(Storming in at the commotion):

I thought I told you to take her to the Zoo!

FOOTMAN FOOL

I did!
And now, after supper,
I'm taking her to the movies.

<u>END</u>

31209720R00061

Made in the USA
Middletown, DE
22 April 2016